Comparing Bugs

Bug Senses

Charlotte Guillain

Heinemann Library
Chicago, Illinois

www.heinemannraintree.com

Visit our website to find out more information about Heinemann-Raintree books.

To order:

☎ Phone 888-454-2279

💻 Visit www.heinemannraintree.com to browse our catalog and order online.

Edited by Rebecca Rissman and Catherine Veitch
Designed by Joanna Hinton-Malivoire
Picture research by Elizabeth Alexander
Production by Duncan Gilbert and Victoria Fitzgerald
Originated by Heinemann Library
Printed and bound in China by South China Printing Company Ltd

14 13 12 11 10
10 9 8 7 6 5 4 3 2 1

Library of Congress Cataloging-in-Publication Data

Bug senses / Charlotte Guillain. -- 1st ed.
  p. cm. -- (Comparing bugs)
ISBN 978-1-4329-3566-5 (hb) -- ISBN 978-1-4329-3575-7 (pb)
QL467.2.G8567 2010
595.7--dc22

                    2009025546

Acknowledgments
The author and publishers are grateful to the following for permission to reproduce copyright material: Getty Images p. **21** (DEA / CHRISTIAN RICCI); iStockphoto p. **17**; Photolibrary pp. **6** (Michael Dietrich/ imagebroker.net), **9** (David M Dennis/OSF), **7** (OSF), **14** (Jack Clark/Animals Animals), **15** (Klaus Honal/age footstock), **16** (Herbert Zettl/Cusp), **23 middle** (Jack Clark/Animals Animals), **23 bottom** (Klaus Honal/age footstock); Shutterstock pp. **4** (© Cathy Keifer), **5** (© Anton Chernenko), **18** (© Hway Kiong Lim), **8** (© Kirsanov), **10** (© Tompi), **11** (© Sascha Burkard), **12** (© Neale Cousland), **13** (© Danijel Micka), **19** (© Armin Rose), **20** (© orionmystery@flickr), **22 top left** (© Studio Araminta), **22 bottom left** (© RCL), **22 middle top** (© Vinicius Tupinamba), **22 right** (© Ivelin Radkov), **23 top** (© Neale Cousland).

Cover photograph of a jumping spider reproduced with permission of FLPA (Mark Moffett/Minden Pictures). Back cover photograph of a night butterfly (Actias artemis) reproduced with permission of Shutterstock (© Kirsanov).

The publishers would like to thank Nancy Harris and Kate Wilson for their assistance in the preparation of this book.

Every effort has been made to contact copyright holders of any material reproduced in this book. Any omissions will be rectified in subsequent printings if notice is given to the publisher.

Contents

Meet the Bugs

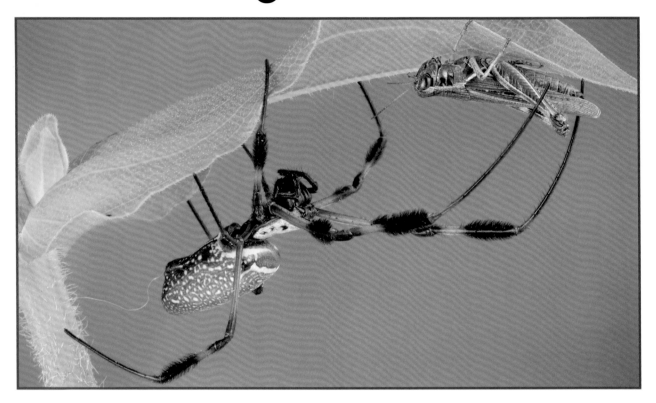

There are many different types
of bugs.

Bugs can smell and taste.

They can also feel, hear, and see.

Smell and Taste

Bugs smell and taste in
different ways.

antennae

Insects use their antennae to smell and taste.

antennae

A moth uses its antennae to smell other bugs.

hairs

A spider uses hairs on its legs to smell other bugs.

tongue

Some insects use their tongues to taste food.

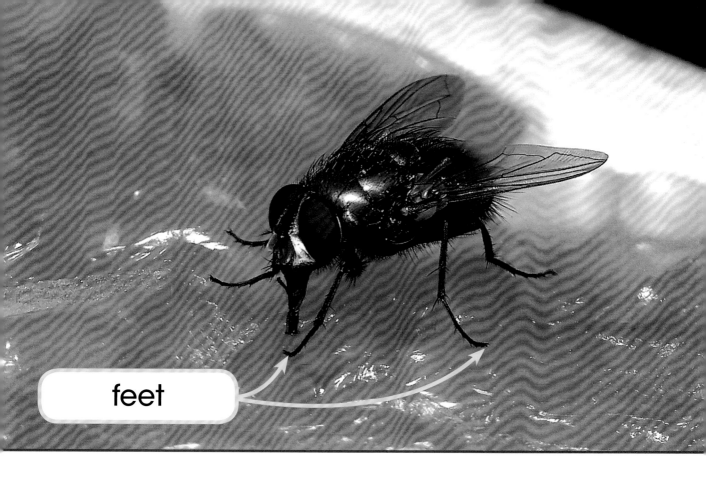

feet

Some insects use their feet to taste food.

Feeling

antennae

Bugs feel in different ways.

Many bugs feel with their antennae.

hairs

Many bugs feel with hairs on
their bodies.

tail

Some bugs feel things moving with their tails.

web

Spiders can feel things moving on their webs.

Hearing

Bugs hear in different ways.
A grasshopper can use its body to
hear things.

A praying mantis can use its body to hear things.

Seeing

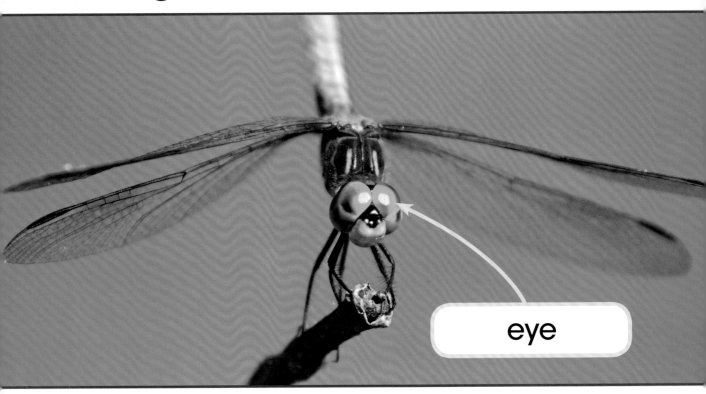

eye

Bugs see in different ways.

Insects have special eyes.

little eyes

Insect eyes are made of many little eyes. Each little eye sees something different.

eyes

Spiders have six or eight eyes.

Earthworms do not have eyes.

How Big?

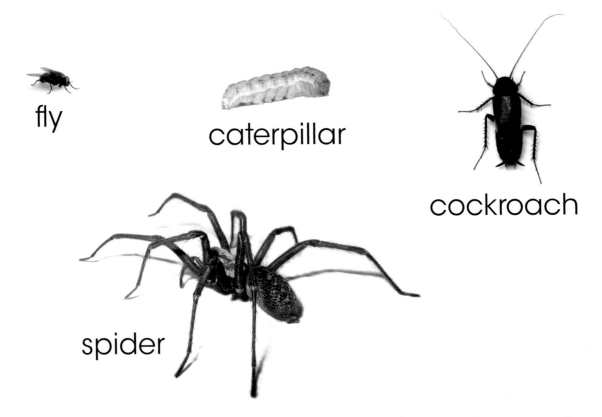

fly

caterpillar

cockroach

spider

Look at how big some of the bugs in this book can be.

Picture Glossary

 **antenna** long, thin feeler on the head of an insect

 **insect** very small creature with six legs

 **web** net that spiders make to catch insects

Index

Notes to Parents and Teachers

Before reading

Make a list of bugs with the children. Try to include insects, arachnids (e.g. spiders), crustaceans (e.g. wood lice), myriapods (e.g. centipedes and millipedes), and earthworms. Ask them if they know what our five senses are. Do they think bugs have the same senses as us? Do they have eyes, ears, noses, or tongues like us?

After reading

- Make bug masks showing eyes and antennae. Ask the children to choose a bug, such as a spider, moth, bee, or dragonfly. Look carefully at pictures of their chosen bugs and discuss the color and number of their eyes. Are they made up of many small eyes? If they have antennae, what are they like? Use index cards, shiny paper and wrappers, tissue paper, and pipe cleaners to make masks of bug faces.
- Between spring and late summer you could go out of the classroom looking for flowers. Which flowers are bees and butterflies visiting? Ask the children to smell and observe the color of these flowers. What do they notice? Help the children to draw up tally charts to record how many flying insects visit each colored flower. Is there a color preference?